TIMELINE HISTORY

HOMES

From Caves to Eco-pods

Elizabeth Raum

www.raintreepublishers.co.uk
Visit our website to find out
more information about
Raintree books.

To order:
☎ Phone 0845 6044371
📠 Fax +44 (0) 1865 312263
✉ Email myorders@raintreepublishers.co.uk

Customers from outside the UK please telephone +44 1865 312262

Raintree is an imprint of Capstone Global Library Limited,
a company incorporated in England and Wales having its
registered office at 7 Pilgrim Street, London, EC4V 6LB
– Registered company number: 6695582

Text © Capstone Global Library Limited 2011
First published in hardback in 2011
The moral rights of the proprietor have been asserted.

Edited by Louise Galpine and Diyan Leake
Designed by Richard Parker
Original illustrations © Capstone Global Library Ltd 2011
Illustrated by Jeff Edwards
Picture research by Hannah Taylor
Originated by Dot Gradations Ltd
Printed and bound in China by CTPS

ISBN 978 0 431 02551 3 (hardback)
14 13 12 11 10
10 9 8 7 6 5 4 3 2 1

British Library Cataloguing in Publication Data
Raum, Elizabeth – Homes : from caves to eco-pods
(Timeline history)
643.1'09-dc22
A full catalogue record for this book is available from the
British Library.

Acknowledgements
We would like to thank the following for permission to
reproduce photographs: Alamy Images pp. **7** top (© RIA
Novosti), **10** top (© Arcticphoto), **12** bottom (© Peter
Horree), **16** (© Anna Stowe), **24** bottom (© View Pictures
Ltd); Corbis pp. **5** (Atlantide Phototravel), **6** (The Gallery
Collection), **11** bottom (Destination), **15** top (Nik Wheeler),
17 top (Edward S. Curtis), **20**, **21** bottom (Reuters/Thomas
Mukoya), **22** (Bettmann), **24** top (Bettmann), **25** (The
Cover Story/Floris Leeuwenberg), **26** bottom (Art on File),
27 (Arcaid/Larraine Worpole); Getty Images pp. **7** bottom
(Riser/Andreas Stirnberg), **12** top (Dea Picture Library),
21 top (Popperfoto), **23** top (Iconica/Superstudio); Mary
Evans Picture Library p. **18**; Photolibrary pp. **4** (Wes Walker),
8 (Dan Gair Photographic), **9** top (Jim Steinberg), **10** bottom
(Michele Falzone), **11** top (Egmont Strigl), **13** top (P. Narayan),
14 (National Trust Photo Library), **15** bottom (Steve Vidler),
17 bottom (M.A. Otsoa de Alda), **19** top (Walter Bibikow),
19 bottom (Raymond Forbes), **23** bottom (Doco Dalfiano);
Rex Features pp. **9** bottom (The Travel Library), **26** top (Yan
Morvan).

Cover photograph of shipping containers being used as
building material for flats, reproduced with permission of
Corbis (Benedict Luxmore).

We would like to thank Ryan Hines for his invaluable help in
the preparation of this book.

Every effort has been made to contact copyright holders
of material reproduced in this book. Any omissions will
be rectified in subsequent printings if notice is given to
the publisher.

Contents

Historical time is divided into two major periods. BC is short for "before Christ" – that is, the time before the Christian religion began. This is the time up to the year 1 BC. AD is short for "Anno Domini". This is Latin for "in the year of our Lord", meaning the time from the year 1 BC to the present. For example, when a date is given as AD 1000, it is 1000 years after the year 1 BC. The abbreviation *c.* stands for *circa*, which is Latin for "around".

Any words appearing in the text in bold, **like this**, are explained in the glossary.

Homes for everyone

Houses shelter us from the weather and protect us while we sleep. In warm climates, houses provide shade. In colder climates, doors, windows, and thick walls protect us from freezing. Throughout history, poor people have built simple homes using materials such as sticks, stones, or mud. Rich and powerful people build bigger homes using costly materials such as cut stone, timber, and steel.

People have lived in these cave homes in Turkey for thousands of years.

This book looks at homes from the earliest days to the present. It cannot include all kinds of houses, of course, but focuses on the different kinds of shelters people use. Houses vary from place to place, but whether we are rich, poor, or in-between, we need homes for shelter and protection.

Timelines

The information in this book is on a timeline. A timeline shows you events from history in the order they happened. The big timeline in the middle of each page gives you details of a certain time in history (see below).

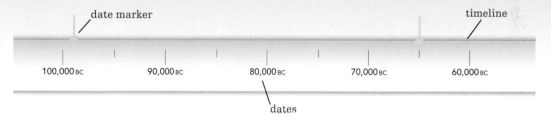

date marker | timeline

100,000 BC   90,000 BC   80,000 BC   70,000 BC   60,000 BC

dates

The dates are not exact because early people did not keep written records. Other dates cover decades or centuries because they show what happened over a general period of time rather than on a precise date. The smaller timeline at the bottom of each page shows you how the page you are reading fits into history as a whole. You will read about homes from all around the world. Each entry on the main timeline is in a different colour. This colour shows you which continent the information is about. The map below shows you how this colour coding works. Pale green indicates events that took place on more than one continent or worldwide.

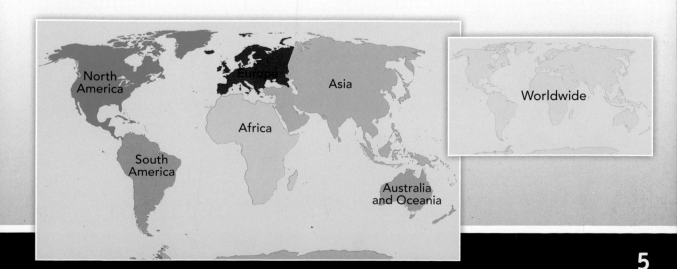

North America

Europe

Asia

Africa

South America

Australia and Oceania

Worldwide

Caves and campsites

Early people found shelter in caves or beneath trees or overhanging rocks. Caves were warm in winter and cool in summer. By about 33,000 BC, people in France began decorating their caves by drawing on the walls. Today, it is thought that over 40 million people throughout the world live in caves. Many have electricity and modern furniture.

*c.*98,000 BC–present

Caves have been used as homes for thousands of years.

*c.*50,000–35,000 BC

Overhanging cliffs or rocks served as shelters while people hunted for game or gathered wild fruit.

100,000 BC   90,000 BC   80,000 BC   70,000 BC   60,000 BC

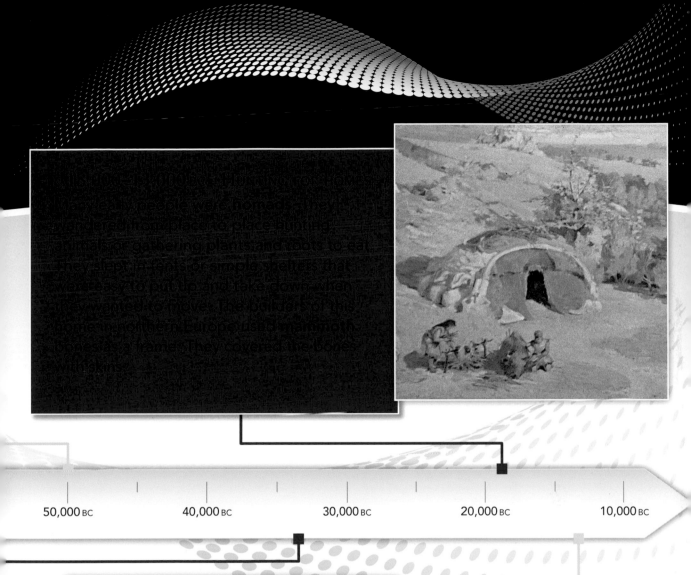

c.35,000–c.13,000 BC Humans took shelter
Many early humans were nomads. They
wandered from place to place, hunting
animals or gathering plants and roots to eat.
They slept in tents or simple shelters that
were easy to put up and take down when
they wanted to move. The builders of this
home in northern Europe used mammoth
bones as a frame. They covered the bones
with skins.

50,000 BC   40,000 BC   30,000 BC   20,000 BC   10,000 BC

*c.*13,000 BC–present
Round huts, made of mud,
stones, or clay, with straw roofs,
have just one room. They are
still used today in many places
in the world.

Using what's available

Around 9000 BC, people began growing crops for food. They settled in one place and built permanent, or lasting, homes. They used whatever building materials were to hand.

c.8000 BC

In Jericho, an ancient city in the **Middle East**, houses were made of stone. Earlier houses were made of mud bricks which softened and collapsed when it rained.

8500 BC		8000 BC		7500 BC		7000 BC		6500 BC		6000 BC	

c.7000 BC   Twigs and mud

Many ancient people in western Asia, central Europe, and North America used **wattle and daub**. Corner posts held up a **thatched** roof of straw or **reeds**. Wattle is a pattern of crossed sticks or twigs. Daub is a mixture of water, mud, straw, and dung (animal waste) used to cover the wattle. The dung holds the mud and straw together so that the mixture lasts.

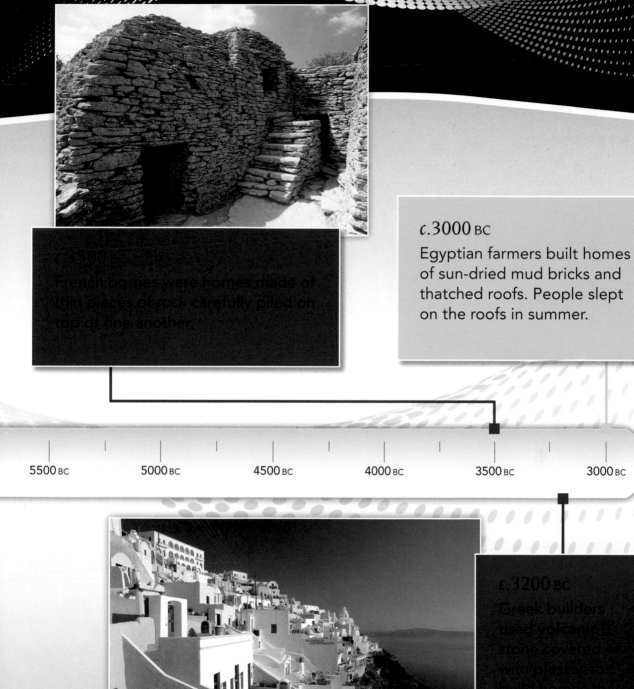

*c.*3500 BC
French *borries* were homes made of thin pieces of rock carefully piled on top of one another.

*c.*3000 BC
Egyptian farmers built homes of sun-dried mud bricks and thatched roofs. People slept on the roofs in summer.

5500 BC   5000 BC   4500 BC   4000 BC   3500 BC   3000 BC

*c.*3200 BC
Greek builders used volcanic stone covered with plaster to build homes that fitted snugly onto cliffs overlooking the sea.

Renewable materials

Early builders made bricks from mud, clay, and straw. They also used **reeds** and grasses. These materials are **renewable**; they replace themselves naturally. If a house needed repairs, fixing it was as easy as stepping outside and gathering more mud, reeds, or straw.

*c.*3000 BC–present

Inuit people in Alaska, Canada, and Russia made iglus (also spelled igloos) from blocks of snow. Iglus are strong structures that protect against cold weather outside while the inside is warmed by people's body heat.

3000 BC | 2750 BC | 2500 BC | 2250 BC | 2000 BC | 1750 BC | 1500 BC

*c.*3000 BC–present

In Peru's lakes and swampy areas, people used reeds to build shelters. The houses are on islands made of woven reeds, which people continue to rebuild today.

c.200 BC–present   Yurts

A yurt is a circular tent built on a frame and covered with felt or animal fur. **Nomads** in Russia, China, and Mongolia lived in yurts. When they moved on, they took the yurt with them. Today, yurts are popular holiday homes in North America, Europe, and in Japan and Korea. Modern yurts have electricity and toilets.

1250 BC   1000 BC   750 BC   500 BC   250 BC   1 BC

c.500 BC–present

Wattle and daub are used like this to make people in the country live on islands throughout Europe.

c.100 BC–present

Bamboo is light, tough, and long lasting. People throughout Asia use it for walls, roofs, floors, and furniture.

Homes to show off

As cities and villages grew, wealthy people built fancy homes to prove that they were important and powerful. Greeks and Romans used large blocks of cut stone, such as **marble** for walls, steps, and even roofs. They also built tall columns, or posts, of polished marble.

c. 600–80 BC PRIVACY
Homes of wealthy Greeks and Romans often had an atrium, or central room with an open roof, surrounded by columns. A pool in the centre caught rainwater. Although they liked privacy at home, Greeks and Romans took baths with friends. Men and women went to separate public bath houses to bathe.

600 BC | 500 BC | 400 BC | 300 BC | 200 BC | 100 BC | 1 BC

AD 200–present
The Toba Batak people of Indonesia built high-roofed houses on **stilts** to avoid getting flooded and to be safe from wild animals.

AD 500–present

The city of Sana'a in Yemen became a major centre in Arabia and, over time, more than 6,000 tower houses were built. Parts of these still exist now. They can be up to nine storeys high and have a flat roof and painted walls.

AD 100 AD 200 AD 300 AD 400 AD 500 AD 600

AD 400s

Rulers of the Ethiopian kingdom of Axum built a castle with stone walls and four corner towers.

AD 600s

In Mexico, Mayan leaders lived in palaces made of cut stone.

Building for protection

Castles were built like forts. The owner and his family lived in a strong stone home called a keep. Some castles included hidden rooms and secret passageways that led from beneath the castle out into the countryside. High stone walls, a water-filled trench called a moat, and a drawbridge protected the castle from attack. The moat stank. Castle toilets emptied directly into it.

1200–1300

Syrian rulers built castles in lonely mountain areas to protect against attack. Underground tunnels allowed those inside to escape.

AD 900   950   1000   1050   1100   1150   1200

AD 900s–1500s
Stone towers and a moat protected the castle's owner from attack.

1200–1300 PUEBLO

The Anasazi people, who lived in the southwestern part of North America, made homes in rock cliffs by adding rooms on to existing caves. This dwelling at Mesa Verde, called the Cliff Palace, had 150 rooms. The location protected it from invaders.

1250	1300	1350	1400	1450	1500

1500s

Matsumoto Castle in Japan was a home for the local lord and his family as well as a fort. It is built on a stone foundation and has three moats.

Dark days and nights

During the Middle Ages (AD 500–1500) most houses were dark inside. Windows were small because glass was expensive and the stone walls could not support large openings without collapsing. Heavy curtains or **shutters** kept the cold out. They kept the light out, too. The only lighting came from the fireplace or candles.

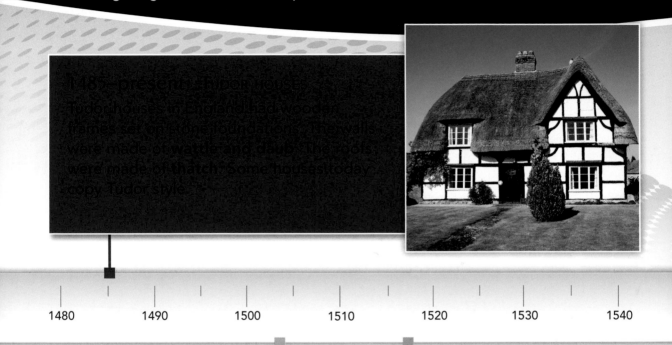

1485–present Tudor house
Tudor houses in England had wooden frames set on stone foundations. The walls were made of wattle and daub. The roofs were made of thatch. Some houses today copy Tudor style.

1480   1490   1500   1510   1520   1530   1540

1500s
In Turkey, many houses had two separate areas – one for family members and one for guests. The family area was called the harem.

1500s
Inca homes in Peru were made of stone and covered with mud or clay. There were no windows.

1600s–early 1900s

A tipi (or tepee) is made of wooden poles covered with animal skins. They can be taken down and moved when necessary. The Blackfeet, Crow, Lakota, and other Native American tribes used tipis.

1550 1560 1570 1580 1590 1600

1500s

Spanish people used paper or the greased skin of a sheep or goat to let light in and keep cold out during the winter. Iron bars on the windows protected the houses from break-ins.

Houses for rich and poor

Rich people lived in palaces and plantations with fancy furniture, while poor people slept on mats in simple huts. If they were lucky, poor families owned a table and one chair for the father. This is where we get the word *chairman* from.

1600s

The Shona people of Zimbabwe lived in small circular huts made of clay. As children grew, they were given smaller huts of their own near by.

1669–1790

The French king's Palace of Versailles, outside Paris, included a hall with 357 costly mirrors.

| 1200 | 1250 | 1300 | 1350 | 1400 | 1450 | 1500 |

1200s–1600 COLD AND SMELLY HOUSES

In Europe's palaces and mansions, fireplaces provided the only heat. They sent smoke and soot through the rooms. People rarely bathed so there were no bathrooms. Most Europeans believed dirt protected their body from illness. Smokey fireplaces and stinky people made for grimey, smelly neighbourhoods.

100,000 BC ⊢

1600s–1800s

A cotton plantation called Boone Hall was built in 1681 near Charleston, South Carolina, USA. The slave-owner's family lived in luxury in the main house.

| 1550 | 1600 | 1650 | 1700 | 1750 | 1800 |

1600s–1800s

Slaves who worked on plantations did not live in the main house. They lived in small brick houses like these on the plantation grounds.

Housing millions

In the mid-1700s, Britain's **Industrial Revolution** brought workers to cities for factory jobs. As cities grew, housing became a serious problem. It remains so today. Half of the world's people live in cities.

1770s

People began to put flush toilets in their homes.

1862

In the United States, people could get land for free as long as they farmed it. The land was called a homestead. Homesteaders often started out living in simple huts made of **turf** or wooden shacks.

1770   1785   1800   1815   1830   1845

1800s–present

Thousands of **immigrants** arrived in the United States needing housing. Blocks of flats called **tenements**, like this one in New York City, quickly became overcrowded and run-down.

1897

Poor people in Brazil started to live in **slums** called *favelas*. Today about 150,000–200,000 people live in a slum called Rocinha.

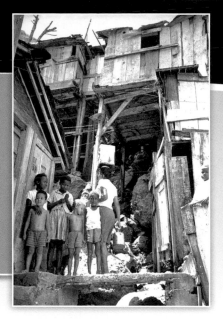

1920s

In Melbourne, Australia, large homes in the city became boarding houses where many families lived together in crowded conditions.

| 1860 | 1875 | 1890 | 1905 | 1920 |

1912–present Slums

A slum was set up in Kenya, where people made houses of tin and **wattle and daub**. Over one million people now live here without electricity, enough water, or **sanitation**. Throughout Kenya, over 2.5 million people live in slum housing. Almost every major city in the world has slum areas.

Suburbs

In the 1950s, middle-class people in Europe and America moved to **suburbs**, neighbourhoods outside cities. They **commuted**, or took cars and trains to work. Today, suburbs surround most of the world's major cities.

1928

In the United States, Willis Carrier invented the "Weathermaker", a home air-conditioner. Air-conditioners began selling well in warmer climates in the 1950s.

1930s

Kitchens became an important part of the house. Before this, kitchens were either outside the house or hidden at the back of the house.

1900   1910   1920   1930   1940   1950

1940s–present   COMFORTABLE HOMES

By the end of World War II in 1945, people wanted comfortable houses with labour-saving appliances. Boilers provided heat. Air-conditioning kept houses cool. Electricity powered lights, televisions, and kitchen appliances. Natural light flowed through big windows. These houses had bathrooms with flush toilets, baths, and showers. Houses were clean and sweet-smelling. People continue to expect these comforts today.

1948

Mobile homes began as camping caravans in the United States. By 1948, many were used as permanent homes. They were up to 9 metres (30 feet) long, and included bathrooms. Today's mobile homes are even larger.

1950s–present

Homes in suburbs, like this one in Brazil, often look very similar.

| 1960 | 1970 | 1980 | 1990 | 2000 |

2000–present

Some suburbs include high-rise apartment blocks like these in Hong Kong's Happy Valley.

One of a kind

Houses in the **suburbs** often looked alike. But some people wanted houses that were one of a kind. **Architects** were happy to take on the challenge by creating brand-new styles.

1956

The design of this house in Caracas, Venezuela includes strong steel beams to prevent it from falling down the hillside.

| 1950 | 1955 | 1960 | 1965 | 1970 | 1975 | 1980 |

1950s GLASS HOUSES

In Britain, Alastair Pilkington invented a new way of making large sheets of flat glass. This made picture windows, skylights, and glass walls possible. Several architects designed houses like this one, built in London in the 1970s, which used large glass sheets. Glass houses seem to disappear into the background. They provide shelter, but not much privacy.

2003

This house in Auroville, India has been built using materials from the past – cloth, mud-baked bricks, and **reed** mats – to create a new style.

1985   1990   1995   2000   2005   2010

1970s

Many people started restoring older houses. Poor areas of cities began to be **gentrified**.

1990s

People in the United States began to build huge houses on small plots of land. Often, there were more bathrooms than bedrooms.

Houses of the future

Maybe one day we'll build homes in outer space or beneath the sea. In the future, builders may return to using materials from the past – **reeds**, mud, and the earth itself – in new and exciting ways.

1990s–present SUSTAINABLE HOUSES

Sustainable or "green" houses use **renewable materials** that can be recycled, and use less energy than other houses. This eco-house in New Mexico, USA is made of tin cans and mud. A wind turbine on the roof and solar panels provide energy. People will build more sustainable houses, or even eco-pods, in the future.

1990

1995

2000

Present

This "air tree" in Madrid, Spain has plants on the inside and solar panels at the top. It provides enough energy to supply electricity to the flats on the estate.

Present

This underground house in Wales uses earth for its roof and walls. Large glass windows provide light and a view of the sea.

2005   2010   Future

Future

Both the United States and China may set up bases on the Moon. Houses on the Moon will have to shelter settlers from temperatures of −233 °Celsius (−387 °Fahrenheit) at night, to 123 °Celsius (253 °Fahrenheit) during the day.

Key dates

98,000 BC–present
Caves are used as homes.

13,000 BC–present
Africans construct one-room huts of mud or clay with straw roofs.

7000 BC–present
Wattle and daub is used in central Europe, western Asia, and North America.

3000 BC
People in Peru use **reeds** to build shelters.

200 BC–present
Nomads in Mongolia, Russia, and China live in yurts.

100 BC–present
Asians use bamboo for walls, roofs, floors, and furniture.

AD 900s–1500s
Castles throughout Europe have stone buildings, towers, and moats to protect their owners.

1200–1300
Syrian rulers build castles in remote mountain areas to protect against attack.

1200–1300
The Anasazi of southwestern North America make homes in rock cliffs by adding rooms onto existing caves.

1485–present
Tudor houses in England are built using wooden frames set on a stone foundation.

1500s
Spanish people use paper or the greased skin of a sheep or goat to let light in and keep cold out during the winter.

1600s–early 1900s
The Blackfeet, Crow, Lakota, and other Native American tribes live in tipis made of wooden poles covered with animal skins.

1770s
People begin to put flush toilets in their homes.

1800s–present
Thousands of **immigrants** in America live in **tenements**.

1880s–present
Slums called *favelas* become places where poor people in Brazil live.

1912–present
Africa's largest slum, in Nairobi, Kenya, is home to over one million people.

1950s
People begin to move to **suburbs** and **commute** to work in cities.

1970s
A process is invented to make large sheets of flat glass for picture windows, skylights, and glass houses.

1970s–present
People start to preserve and restore old homes.

1990s–present
Sustainable houses use less energy. Solar panels or wind turbines create energy to run houses.

Glossary

architect person who designs buildings

commute travel regularly over some distance. People who live in suburbs commute into cities to work.

gentrify change a house or area that is poor or run-down so that it looks nicer

immigrant person who comes to live permanently in a foreign country

Industrial Revolution time of rapid growth of factories that began in England in the mid-1700s and spread to many other countries

mammoth large, elephant-like mammal that used to roam the Earth

marble type of stone used for building that can be polished and comes in a variety of colours

Middle East region that includes south-west Asia and north-east Africa

nomad someone who moves from place to place

plaster thin paste spread on walls

reed straight stalk of grass

renewable material material that comes from a source that will not run out

replica exact copy

sanitation disposal of sewage and human waste

shutter movable cover for a window. Shutters are often made of wood.

slum thickly populated, run-down part of a city, where poor people live

stilt post supporting a structure built above the surface of land or water

suburb community built outside the city

sustainable saves energy and uses renewable materials. Sustainable houses may use energy from the Sun.

tenement run-down and often overcrowded flats, specifically in the United States

thatch material such as straw, rushes, or leaves used to cover roofs

turf surface of the ground covered with grass. Turf houses are built in places where there are no trees that can be used for building material.

volcanic material left after a volcano erupts

wattle and daub building material of interwoven twigs plastered with mud or clay

Find out more

Books

The Amazing World of Castles: Discover the Fascinating History of Medieval Adventure, Battles and Romance, Barbara Taylor (Southwater, 2008)

Building Houses **(Ways into Technology series)**, Richard and Louise Spilsbury (Franklin Watts, 2008)

Home Life: Learn About Houses, Homes and What People Ate in the Past, with 30 Easy-to-make Projects and Recipes **(Hands-on History Projects series)**, Rachel Halstead and Struan Reid (Southwater, 2009)

Home, Family and Everyday Life Through the Ages, John Haywood (Southwater, 2008)

Houses and Homes **(History from Photographs series)**, Pat Hughes and Kath Cox (Wayland, 2006)

Victorian Homes **(Life in the Past series)**, Mandy Ross (Heinemann Library, 2005)

Websites

Click on "Greeks at home" to learn about how houses were built in ancient Greece.
www.bbc.co.uk/schools/primaryhistory/ancient_greeks/home_life

Find out about how the ancient Romans heated their houses and kept their towns clean. Go to the "Fun facts" to learn more about their building skills.
www.bbc.co.uk/schools/primaryhistory/romans/technology

Check out a list and some pictures of the most expensive houses in the world.
home.howstuffworks.com/home-improvement/decorating/most-expensive-houses.htm

An alien called Gleep helps Josie step back into a house in Victorian times.
www.bbc.co.uk/education/dynamo/history/stepback.shtml

Index